FIELD WORK

FIELD WORK

modern poems from eastern forests

edited by
ERIK REECE

THE UNIVERSITY PRESS OF KENTUCKY

Published by The University Press of Kentucky
Scholarly publisher for the Commonwealth, serving Bellarmine University,
Berea College, Centre College of Kentucky, Eastern Kentucky University,
The Filson Historical Society, Georgetown College, Kentucky Historical Society,
Kentucky State University, Morehead State University, Murray State University,
Northern Kentucky University, Transylvania University, University of Kentucky,
University of Louisville, and Western Kentucky University.

Editorial and Sales Offices: The University Press of Kentucky
663 South Limestone Street, Lexington, Kentucky 40508-4008
www.kentuckypress.com

12   11   10   09   08   5   4   3   2   1

Library of Congress Cataloging-in-Publication Data

Field work : modern poems from eastern forests / edited by Erik Reece.
p. cm.
Includes bibliographical references.
ISBN 978-0-8131-2497-1 (acid-free paper) 1. Nature—poetry. 2. American poetry—
20th century. 3. American poetry—East (U.S.) I. Reece, Erik.
PS595.N22F54 2008
811′.5408036—dc22

                                                                    2007052387

This book is printed on acid-free recycled paper meeting
the requirements of the American National Standard
for Permanence in Paper for Printed Library Materials.

Manufactured in the United States of America.

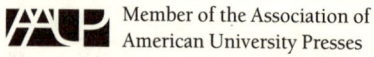   Member of the Association of
American University Presses

to the men and women who fight every day for justice in the coal fields of Appalachia

CONTENTS

Part II

INTRODUCTION

Last year, climatologists found record-high levels of carbon dioxide in the atmosphere. Most people, with the unfortunate exception of some high-placed American politicians, understand that CO_2 is the leading cause of catastrophic, global climate change. At the same time, the greatest consumers of CO_2—trees—are disappearing fast. Forests worldwide have dwindled from about 12 billion acres at the beginning of the century to about 7 billion acres now. In central Appalachia, where I live, over two thousand square miles of forest will be eliminated over the next decade if coal companies continue strip-mining at current levels. Across the United States, such practices have already destroyed 5 million acres. This mining, along with irresponsible logging, has created radical forest fragmentation throughout the world. We have literally marooned many species of flora and fauna inside these forest islands, and many are not surviving. Twelve percent of the world's birds are endangered, as are 24 percent of its mammals and 30 percent of its fish. Edward O. Wilson estimates that if our current levels of consumption continue, 50 percent of all plant and animal species will be gone by 2050. "We and the rest of life cannot afford another hundred years like [the twentieth century]," he concluded in his 2002 book, *The Future of Life*.

Given these alarming—not alarmist—numbers, it is disturbing to realize how few contemporary poets take the natural world as the starting place for their poems. Too often in American poetry, a natural image is only an ornament, a flourish, a stand-in for some emotional abstraction. But in a letter-poem to Carolyn Kizer following an alcoholic meltdown, Richard Hugo suggests where great poetry should come from:

> Dear Condor: Much thanks for that telephonic support
> from North Carolina when I suddenly went ape
> in the Iowa tulips. Lord, but I'm ashamed.
> I was afraid, it seemed, according to the doctor
> of impending success, winning some poetry prizes
> or getting a wet kiss. . . .
>
> . . . .
>
> . . . I'm o.k. now.
> I'm back at the primal source of poems: wind, sea,
> and rain, the market and the salmon.

Getting back to the primal sources of poetry is the reason behind this anthology of poems from the eastern broadleaf forests. I have my own reasons for such a return.

I spent most of 2004 writing a book called *Lost Mountain: A Year in the Vanishing Wilderness,* about a nefarious form of strip-mining called mountaintop removal. As the name implies, entire mountaintops are blasted off every day across Appalachia. The debris is dumped down into headwater valleys, where streams are buried and polluted with heavy metals and sulfuric acid, all in an effort to extract a thin seam of coal in the fastest, cheapest way possible. Mountaintop removal has destroyed so many ridgetops across Kentucky, West Virginia, Virginia, and Tennessee that the state of Delaware could be parceled out and relocated on these former summits. In 2004, I spent more time than I ever wanted to exploring strip mines, flying over them, and talking with people whose homes and lives have been damaged by mountaintop removal. Many times, I stood in the middle of a strip mine site and could not see one living thing. All of this is to say that I spent a year exploring and describing one of the ugliest landscapes and one of the ugliest practices you will ever see. At the end of that year, as a kind of balancing act, I felt a strong need to contribute something beautiful to the world. The result is this collection of poems by poets who still understand the natural world to be an unroofed church, a place of reverence.

I have set the following geographical and historical limits to *Field Work*. All of the poems in the longest section of the book, Part II, were written after World War II. Robert Frost's "The Oven Bird," which serves as a prelude to this collection, was written earlier, in 1916. Its final lines, "The question that he frames in all but words / Is what to make of a diminished thing" presents the inquiry taken up, in different ways, by all of the other poets gathered here. I have chosen post–World War II poems for the body of the book because the real and the psychic landscape of America has been altered so dramatically during the second half of the twentieth century. When Dwight Eisenhower initiated the interstate highway system, those freeways not only eliminated huge tracts of wilderness, but also made it much easier to transport consumer goods. Since then, the rate at which Americans consume has quadrupled, resulting in far fewer forests, many contaminated rivers, poor air quality, and a global climate crisis. Poets may or may not be, as Shelley famously claimed, the "unacknowledged legislators of the world," but in such a critical time as ours, I believe it is urgent that we listen to what some important modern poets have to tell us about natural landscapes.

The geographical limitations I have imposed on this collection—poems only from the eastern side of the Mississippi River—leaves out great American poets of the natural world such as Richard Hugo, W. S. Merwin, William Stafford, Gary Snyder, and Pattiann Rogers. However, in Part I of this anthology I have included some ancient Chinese poets who had no idea that the continent of North America existed at all. Several factors informed this decision. Some years ago, while I was educating myself on the natural history of Appalachia, I was struck by a minor epiphany: the forests of Appalachia are almost identical to those of southern China where some of the first great nature poets—Wang Wei, Li Po, Tu Fu, Han Shan—wrote their famous poems about cascading waterfalls and full moons. Two-thirds of all the wild orchids in Appalachia are cousins to those in China. There are only two species of tulip poplar in the world—one in China and one in the eastern United States. In both forests, the non-woody plants have developed underground storage systems, and most of them bloom in early spring, before the canopy closes over them. Inspect the forest floor in southern China and Appalachia, and you will find the same mayapple, jack-in-the-pulpit, ginseng, and ferns. Apparently, what connects these two ecosystems on opposite sides of the globe is that neither suffered extensive glaciation during the Pleistocene Era. When the ice withdrew, only these two regions retained the plant diversity that was once characteristic of each entire continent.

When I learned this, it suddenly made sense why the American poets I most admire so often remind me of China's Late T'ang masters. Both were responding to the same landscape, and in similar ways. For the ancient Chinese poets, just paying attention to the particular elements of a mountain landscape, and naming those particulars, was often enough. It is as if the poet and the natural world met halfway in the poem's images so that the reader could feel the intensity of a pure, unmitigated experience. In addition, those images often become thresholds back into a natural world we are often too distracted to see. This is, above all, a poetry of belonging, a poetry of elemental contact with something much larger than the self. Many of the poems in this book ask the reader to turn away from virtual, urban landscapes so that she or he might truly *see* the natural world again, and perhaps understand that it is a spectacular, poetic organism.

The Chinese poets I have included in Part I of *Field Work* produced what many today consider the first great "nature writing." Consequently, their work has inspired many of the American poets in Part II to follow in the tradition of *shan-shui,* "river and mountain" poetry. Throughout *Field Work,* poets such as Hayden Carruth, Mary Oliver, and Charles Wright make explicit reference to these poets and this tradition. David Budbill's poetic persona even assumes the name of his native mountain in homage to the Chinese sage Cold Mountain (Han Shan). Poets from the Eastern tradition spoke with reverence of the natural world's "ten thousand things." The Western poets gathered in *Field Work* share that reverence for their own natural landscapes, and their praise is at times coupled with critique of the Western rationalist tradition that has too often dismissed the natural world as merely a resource. American readers are fortunate that two American poets, Kenneth Rexroth and David Hinton, have translated the 1,300-year-old poems so successfully into a modern, free verse idiom.

I have also chosen the Mississippi River as the western boundary for these poems because the eastern United States has its own unique geography, its own cultures, its own ways of thinking and writing—the tendency toward elegy, for instance—that make it quite distinct from the western half of the country. I would like for *Field Work* to reflect that distinction in terms of both its natural and its human history.

A last, more (literally) pedestrian reason for only eliciting poets from eastern landscapes is that this book is meant to fit inside a walker's back pocket, and therefore must be modest in scale and scope. *Field Work* is modeled after the rugged orange field books that foresters carry into the woods to record their observations and research data. It is ready for travel.

While *Field Work* is subtitled *Modern Poems from Eastern Forests*, readers will notice at times what naturalists call an "edge effect"—that is, some of these poems range free of the forest, into surrounding fields and wetlands. John Lane's "The Homecoming of Osceola" is one such poem. It recounts the story of the great Seminole chief's deportation to Edisto Island, South Carolina, because, of all the North American tribes, the Seminole alone refused to sign away their land in a treaty with the Americans. Recently, I traveled through the area of south Florida where Osceola's people lived. With its canals, highways, strip malls, and gated communities, it looks almost entirely like a manmade environment. And there are cars everywhere. Indeed, south Florida looks as if it were designed exclusively *for* the car. But the economic system that created this landscape has also created the carbon dioxide emissions that may sink it. In his film *An Inconvenient Truth*, Al Gore showed a startling graphic of what south Florida would look like if Greenland melted or slipped into the sea. It would all be underwater.

In his great country song "Seminole Wind," John Anderson laments sitting on a cypress stump and listening "to the ghost of Osceola cry." When it comes to the natural world, that native ghost, that voice, might teach us some much-needed lessons about humility, responsibility, and reverence. I like to think the irrepressible spirit of Osceola speaks through many of the poems gathered here as well, and it seems to me that a cypress stump might be a fitting place to read them.

Of course, reading *Field Work* in the *shade* of a cypress tree, or any tree, would be even better. Wendell Berry wrote of his beautiful collection *A Timbered Choir*, "These poems were written in silence, in solitude, mainly out of doors. A reader will like them best, I think, who reads them in similar circumstances." Some of those poems are collected here, and all of the poetry that follows will benefit from similar treatment. The real poem, as Walt Whitman reminds us, begins at the edge of the page. But I hope these pages will assist readers in seeing that real poem with a renewed clarity and intensity. And I hope these pages will remind the reader that the Poem of Creation is an imperiled, but still inspiring scripture—one worth fighting to preserve.

Robert Frost

THE OVEN BIRD

There is a singer everyone has heard,
Loud, a mid-summer and a mid-wood bird,
Who makes the solid tree trunks sound again.
He says that leaves are old and that for flowers
Mid-summer is to spring as one to ten.
He says the early petal-fall is past
When pear and cherry bloom went down in showers
On sunny days a moment overcast;
And comes that other fall we name the fall.
He says the highway dust is over all.
The bird would cease and be as other birds
But that he knows in singing not to sing.
The question that he frames in all but words
Is what to make of a diminished thing.

PART I

Li Po

LISTENING TO LU TZU-HSÜN PLAY THE *CH'IN* ON A MOONLIT NIGHT

The night's lazy, the moon bright. Sitting
here, a recluse plays his pale white *ch'in*,

and suddenly, as if cold pines were singing,
it's all those harmonies of grieving wind.

Intricate fingers flurries of white snow,
empty thoughts emerald-water clarities:

No one understands now. Those who could
hear a song this deeply vanished long ago.

Translated by David Hinton

GAZING AT THE THATCH-HUT MOUNTAIN WATERFALL

I

Climbing west toward Incense-Burner Peak,
I look south and see a falls of water, a cascade

hanging there, three thousand feet high,
then seething dozens of miles down canyons.

Sudden as lightning breaking into flight,
its white rainbow of mystery appears. Afraid

at first the celestial Star River is falling,
splitting and dissolving into cloud heavens,

I look up into force churning in strength,
all power, the very workings of Change-Maker.

It keeps ocean winds blowing ceaselessly,
shines a mountain moon back into empty space,

empty space it tumbles and sprays through,
rinsing green cliffs clean on both sides,

sending pearls in flight scattering into mist
and whitewater seething down towering rock.

Here, after wandering among these renowned
mountains, the heart grows rich with idleness.

Why talk of cleansing elixirs of immortality?
Here, the world's dust rinsed from my face,

I'll stay close to what I've always loved,
content to leave that peopled world forever.

2

Sunlight on Incense-Burner kindles violet smoke.
Watching the distant falls hanging there, river

headwaters plummeting three thousand feet in flight,
I see the Star River falling through nine heavens.

Translated by David Hinton

LISTENING TO A MONK'S *CH'IN* DEPTHS

Carrying a *ch'in* cased in green silk, a monk
descended from Eyebrow Mountain in the west.

When he plays, even in a few first notes,
I hear the pines of ten thousand valleys,

and streams rinse my wanderer's heart clean.
Echoes linger among temple frost-fall bells,

night coming unnoticed in emerald mountains,
autumn clouds banked up, gone dark and deep.

Translated by David Hinton

Tu Fu

WRITTEN ON THE WALL AT CHANG'S HERMITAGE

It is Spring in the mountains.
I come alone seeking you.
The sound of chopping wood echoes
Between the silent peaks.
The streams are still icy.
There is snow on the trail.
At sunset I reach your grove
In the stony mountain pass.
You want nothing, although at night
You can see the aura of gold
And silver ore all around you.
You have learned to be gentle
As the mountain deer you have tamed.
The way back forgotten, hidden
Away, I become like you,
An empty boat, floating, adrift.

Translated by Kenneth Rexroth

REFLECTIONS IN AUTUMN

Jade-pure dew wounds maple forests, Shaman Mountain
forests rising from Shaman Gorge, *ch'i*-wind heaving.

The river's billows and waves breach skies churning.
Clouds drift above passes, touching darkness to earth.

Chrysanthemum blossoms have opened tears here twice:
my lost lives, my lone boat moored to a homesick heart. . . .

Everywhere, urgently, winter clothes are cut to pattern.
Fulling-stone rhythms fill the air, tightening at twilight.

Translated by David Hinton

DAWN LANDSCAPE

The last watch has sounded in K'uei-chou.
Color spreading above Solar-Terrace Mountain,

a cold sun clears high peaks. Clouds linger,
blotting out canyons below tangled ridges,

and deep Yangtze banks keep sails hidden.
Beneath clear skies: clatter of falling leaves.

And these deer at my bramble gate: so close
here, we touch our own kind in each other.

Translated by David Hinton

Wang Wei

IN REPLY TO VICE-MAGISTRATE CHANG

In these twilight years, I love tranquillity
alone. Mind free of our ten thousand affairs,

self-regard free of all those grand schemes,
I return to my old forest, knowing empty.

Soon mountain moonlight plays my *ch'in*.
Pine woods loosen my robes. Explain this

inner pattern behind failure and success?
Fishing song carries into shoreline depths.

Translated by David Hinton

BIRD AND WATERFALL MUSIC

Men sleep. The cassia blossoms fall.
The Spring night is still in the empty mountains.
When the full moon rises,
It troubles the wild birds.
From time to time you can hear them
Above the sound of the flooding waterfalls.

Translated by Kenneth Rexroth

WITH FRIENDS ON SHEN'S SUTRA-STUDY TERRACE, NEW BAMBOO SPROUTING

In this idleness, quiet clarity deepens
each day, tall bamboo graceful of itself,

lush. Tender joints cling to dry sheaths
where new thickets grace the old fence,

and as wind clamors in slender branches
shadow scatters through cold moonlight.

They're harvested for fishing poles and
dragon flutes—but inside the gate of Way,

how could such things rival kingfisher-
green sweeping timeless altars of stone?

Translated by David Hinton

Han Shan (Cold Mountain)

I delight in the everyday Way, myself
among mist and vine, rock and cave,

wildlands feeling so boundlessly free,
white clouds companions in idleness.

Roads don't reach those human realms.
You only climb this high in no-mind:

I sit here on open rock: a lone night,
a full moon drifting up Cold Mountain.

Translated by David Hinton

I've lived out tens of thousands of years
on Cold Mountain. Given to the seasons,

I vanished among forests and cascades,
gazed into things so utterly themselves.

No one ventures up into all these cliffs
hidden forever in white mist and cloud.

It's just me, thin grass my sleeping mat
and azure heaven my comforting quilt:

happily pillowed on stone, I'm given to
heaven and earth changing on and on.

Translated by David Hinton

The cloud road's choked with deep mist. No one gets here that way,
but these Heaven-Terrace Mountains have always been my home:

a place to vanish among five-thousand-foot cliffs and pinnacles,
ten thousand creeks and gorges all boulder towers and terraces.

I follow streams in birch-bark cap, wooden sandals, tattered robes,
and clutching a goosefoot walking-stick, circle back around peaks.

Once you realize this floating life is the perfect mirage of change,
it's breathtaking—this wild joy at wandering boundless and free.

Translated by David Hinton

PART II

James Still

WHEN THE DULCIMERS ARE GONE

When the dulcimers are mingled with the dust
Of flowering chestnut, and their lean fretted necks
Are slain maple stalks, their strings dull threads of rust,
Where shall the mellow voice be heard upon the hills,
Upon what pennyroyal meadow, beside what rills?

Where shall the gentle words in mild abandon sing
With sweet design in loitering melody
As flights of swallows aimless on the wing,
Yet skilled as scythes that curve through yellow grain
And fragrant as jasmine after freshening rain?

Or may the heart's breath on the slender reed
Sing bright virelays to match the oriole?—
The tulip tree the lyre that one must heed
When the dulcimers are gone, when afternoons attend
The silver underleaf of poplars in the wind?

WILDERNESS

Need the words unspoken be said here
Under the red maples, in a vale of trees
Piercing the clay and rancid sodden leaves
Dyed with madder?
                          Or under the green cedars
On the hill's saddle?

Let not a word fall on pale strawberry blossoms
Beneath the lynn tree's vagrant whispering,
Or a syllable bleed on spikes of cinnamon fern,—
All speech made here will know an early withering.

In the cool stillness where shadow-flowers dance
Lean poplars will flaunt all thoughts that burn
Into futile words within a haughty wilderness.
All beauty here that trudges hills and skies
Is clothed in silence and in silence dies.

HERITAGE

I shall not leave these prisoning hills
Though they topple their barren heads to level earth
And the forests slide uprooted out of the sky.
Though the waters of Troublesome, of Trace Fork,
Of Sand Lick rise in a single body to glean the valleys,
To drown lush pennyroyal, to unravel rail fences;
Through the sun-ball breaks the ridges into dust
And burns its strength into the blistered rock
I cannot leave. I cannot go away.

Being of these hills, being one with the fox
Stealing into the shadows, one with the new-born foal,
The lumbering ox drawing green beech logs to mill,
One with the destined feet of man climbing and descending,
And one with death rising to bloom again, I cannot go.
Being of these hills I cannot pass beyond.

I WAS BORN HUMBLE

I was born humble. At the foot of the mountains
My face was set upon the immensity of earth
And stone; and upon oaks full-bodied and old.
There is so much writ upon the parchment of leaves,
So much of beauty blown upon the winds,
I can but fold my hands and sink my knees
In the leaf-pages. Under the mute trees
I have cried with this scattering of knowledge,
Beneath the flight of birds shaken with this waste
Of wings.
        I was born humble. My heart grieves
Beneath this wealth of wisdom perished with the leaves.

HILL-LONELY

These were your hills, these your foggy coves
Beneath the mountain's shadowing arms
Lifting skyward where white moonlight roves
Silent as fox feet.

                 These were sheltering ridges
Against long waiting, against the heart's alarms,
Against the lengthening agony of an anxious day.

Call out of yesterday, speak to the voiceless hills
Within your heart: call to the emptiness of level earth
To lift its shoulders upward until it fills
The vast untended acres of the blossoming sky,
Until the poplars stand at angles on the mountain's girth
And throw a mellow shade to cool a throbbing brow.

EPITAPH FOR UNCLE IRA COMBS, MOUNTAIN PREACHER

So long on mountains he had looked,
All earth was dull that did not tower up
Into the sky.
                        So long upon the hills
Of faith his soul had calmly leaned,
He was a bulwark firm within his God,
A mountain rising high.

RIVER OF EARTH

The sea saw it and fled. . . .
The mountains skipped like rams, and the little hills like lambs.

He drank the bright air into his throat
And cast a glance across the shattered thrust
Of hills: And he knew that of all men who slept,
Who waked suddenly, he least of all could name this thing
That held them here. He least could put the sound
Upon his tongue and build the spoken words
That all might know, might speak themselves, might write
In flowing script for those who come upon this place
In curious search, knowing this land for what it is.

But there are those who learn what is told here
By convolutions of earth, by time, by winds,
The water's wearings and minute shapings of man.
They have struck pages with the large print of knowledge,
The thing laid open, the hills translated.
He least can know of this.

                    He can but stand
A stranger on familiar slopes and drink the restless air,
Knowing that beneath his feet, beneath his probing eyes
A river of earth flows down the strident centuries.

Hills are but waves cast up to fall again, to rise
Still further down the years.

                              Men are held here
Within a mighty tide swept onward toward a final sea.

James Wright

MARCH

A bear under the snow
Turns over to yawn.
It's been a long, hard rest.

Once, as she lay asleep, her cubs fell
Out of her hair,
And she did not know them.

It is hard to breathe
In a tight grave:

So she roars,
And the roof breaks.
Dark rivers and leaves
Pour down.

When the wind opens its doors
In its own good time,
The cubs follow that relaxed and beautiful woman
Outside to the unfamiliar cities
Of moss.

AMERICAN WEDDING

She dreamed long of waters.
Inland today, she wakens
On scraped knees, lost
Among locust thorns.

She gropes for
The path backward, to
The pillows of the sea.

Bruised trillium
Of wilderness, she
May rest on briar leaves,
As long as the wind cares to pause.

Now she is going to learn
How it is that animals
Can save time:
They sleep a whole season
Of lamentation and snow,
Without bothering to weep.

LATE NOVEMBER IN A FIELD

Today I am walking alone in a bare place,
And winter is here.
Two squirrels near a fence post
Are helping each other drag a branch
Toward a hiding place; it must be somewhere
Behind those ash trees.
They are still alive, they ought to save acorns
Against the cold.
Frail paws rifle the troughs between cornstalks when the moon
Is looking away.
The earth is hard now,
The soles of my shoes need repairs.
I have nothing to ask a blessing for,
Except these words.
I wish they were
Grass.

Lorine Niedecker

Black Hawk held: In reason
land cannot be sold,
only things to be carried away,
and I am old.

Young Lincoln's general moved,
pawpaw in bloom,
and to this day, Black Hawk,
reason has small room.

July, waxwings
on the berries
have dyed red
          the dead
branch

The death of my poor father
leaves debts
and two small houses.

To settle this estate
a thousand fees arise—
I enrich the law.

Before my own death is certified,
recorded, final judgment
judged

taxes taxed
I shall own a book
of old Chinese poems

and binoculars
to probe the river
trees.

He lived—childhood summers
        thru bare feet
then years of money's lack
        and heat

beside the river—out of flood
        came his wood, dog,
woman, lost her, daughter—
        prologue

to planting trees. He buried carp
        beneath the rose
where grass-still
        the marsh rail goes.

To bankers on high land
        he opened his wine tank.
He wished his only daughter
        to work in the bank

but he'd given her a source
        to sustain her—
a weedy speech,
        a marshy retainer.

A. R. Ammons

DELAWARE WATER GAP

Rounding the mountain's rim-ledge,
we looked out valleyward
onto the summits of lesser hills,

summits bottoms of held air, still lesser
heights clefts and ravines: oh, I said,
the land's a slow ocean, the long blue

ridge a reared breakage, these small peaks
dips and rises: we're floating,
I said, intermediates of stone and air,

and nothing has slowed altogether
into determination and a new wave
to finish this one is building up somewhere,

a continent crowded loose, upwarping
against its suasions, we, you and I,
to be drowned, now so sustained and free.

COMING ROUND

The oar squeaks,
a dash sound like
moon-hustle on the river:

reeds
trap and ease the
boat slow

to ripple-tilting sanddown:
the night, a
bubble,

hangs two hundred
thousand miles by
a moon-filament:

I tie up, head for the single
windowlight:
I cut the moon free.

RAPIDS

Fall's leaves are redder than
spring's flowers, have no pollen,
and also sometimes fly, as the wind
schools them out or down in shoals
or droves: though I
have not been here long, I can
look up at the sky at night and tell
how things are likely to go for
the next hundred million years:
the universe will probably not find
a way to vanish nor I
in all that time reappear.

MOUNTAIN WIND

I went out into the cancellations of the wind
and stood still
my arms up stiff
like shrubs

Oh I said I have discovered my consequence
This celebration of
water and lust is not
my celebration but a speech

the deep says and sends the wind through
I touched the sharp tips
of stalks and stood in the lone
hurry of time down the mountain slope

Hayden Carruth

PARTICULARITY

How it is blurring, oozing
        slowly away from
me. This is an
        awful moment

every time. The grove
        of sumac I've known
so long becoming
        a lump of

undifferentiated land-
        scape, like the fallen
barn and the hill
        itself. Then

everything is one,
        is nothing. Only
here is left, here—
        this invisible

hereness where I am,
        where I am
existing, here, the center
        of mystery.

THE BROOK

Murmuring of the brook in late
summer darkness, after moonset,
as I lay sleepless on the porch cot.
A music extraordinarily variable.
Each passage of water against its stone
sounding a different pitch and rhythm.
It was an uncivilized music in the
foothills of the mountains, continuing
long beyond the endurance of a human
singer, almost beyond the endurance
of a human listener, syllables
of unknown meaning, notes on an
unknown scale. A few fat yellow
stars above the northern horizon.
Without art, the song was perfectly
artistic. The unmeaning music
and the unknowing listener were one
in the loneliness of those distant
late summer nights in Vermont.
Truly the music meant nothing,
no intimation, which was why
I liked it so much, my brook
murmuring all night in the darkness,
and I meant nothing, and I liked that too.

THE RAVINE

Stones, brown tufted grass, but no water,
it is dry to the bottom. A seedy eye
of orange hawkweed blinks in sunlight
stupidly, a mink bumbles away,
a ringnecked snake among stones lifts its head
like a spark, a dead young woodcock—
long dead, the mink will not touch it—
sprawls in the hatchment of its soft plumage
and clutches emptiness with drawn talons.
This is the ravine today. But in spring it
cascaded, in water it filled with snow
until it lay hidden completely. In time,
geologic time, it will melt away
or deepen beyond recognition, a huge
gorge. These are what I remember and foresee.
These are what I see here every day,
not things but relationships of things,
quick changes and slow. These are my sorrow,
for unlike my bright admonitory friends
I see relationships, I do not see things.
These, such as they are, every day, every
unique day, the first in time and the last,
are my thoughts, the sequences of my mind.
I wonder what they mean. Every day,
day after day, I wonder what they mean.

THE POET

All night his window
shines in the woods
shadowed under the hills
where the gray owl

is hunting. He hears
the woodmouse scream—
so small a sound
in the great darkness

entering his pain.
For he is all and all
of pain, attracting
every new injury

to be taken and borne
as he must take
and bear it. He is
nothing; he is

his admiration. So
they seem almost
to know—the woodmouse
and the roving owl,

the woods and hills.
All night they move
around the stillness
of the poet's light.

OF DISTRESS BEING HUMILIATED BY THE CLASSICAL CHINESE POETS

Masters, the mock orange is blooming in Syracuse without scent,
        having been bred by patient horiculturists
To make this greater display at the expense of fragrance.
But I miss the jasmine of my back-country home.
Your language has no tenses, which is why your poems can never
        be translated whole into English;
Your minds are the minds of men who feel and imagine
        without time.

The serenity of the present, the repose of my eyes in the cool
        whiteness of sterile flowers.
Even now the headsman with his great curved blade and rank odor
        is stalking the byways for some of you.
When everything happens at once, no conflicts can occur.
Reality is an impasse. Tell me again
How the white heron rises from the reeds and flies forever
        across the nacreous river at twilight
Toward the distant islands.

Denise Levertov

TRAGIC ERROR

The earth is the Lord's, we gabbled,
and the fullness thereof—
while we looted and pillaged, claiming indemnity:
the fullness thereof
given over to us, to our use—
while we preened ourselves, sure of our power,
wilful or ignorant, through the centuries.

Miswritten, misread, that charge:
subdue was the false, the misplaced word in the story.
Surely we were to have been
earth's mind, mirror, reflective source.
Surely our task
was to have been
to love the earth,
to *dress and keep it* like Eden's garden.

That would have been our *dominion:*
to be those cells of earth's body that could
perceive and imagine, could bring the planet
into the haven it is to be known,
(as the eye blesses the hand, perceiving
its form and the work it can do).

THE LIFE OF OTHERS

Their high pitched baying
as if in prayer's unison

remote, undistracted, given over
utterly to belief.

the skein of geese
voyages south,
            hierarchic arrow of its convergence toward
            the point of grace
swinging and rippling, ribbon tail
of a kite, loftily

over lakes where they have not
elected to rest,

over men who suppose
earth is man's over golden earth

preparing itself
for night and winter.
            We humans
are smaller than they, and crawl
unnoticed,

about and about the smoky map.

THE COMING FALL

The eastern sky at sunset taking
The glow of the west:
           the west a clear stillness.

The east flinging
nets of cloud
to hold the rose light a moment longer:
               the western hill dark to blackness.

The ants
on their acropolis
prepare for the night.

The vine among the rocks
heavy with grapes

the shadows of September
among the gold glint of the grass

among shining
willow leaves the small birds moving

silent in the presence of a new season.

          . . . .

In the last sunlight
human figures dark on the hill
outlined—
a fur of gold
about their shoulders and heads,
a blur defining them.

    . . . .

Down by the fallen fruit in the old orchard
the air grows cold. The hill
hides the sun.

A sense of the present
rises out of earth and grass,
enters the feet, ascends

into the genitals, constricting
the breast, lightening
the head—a wisdom,

a shiver, a delight
that what is passing

is here, as if
a snake went by, green in the
gray leaves.

Wendell Berry

THE WILD GEESE

Horseback on Sunday morning,
harvest over, we taste persimmon
and wild grape, sharp sweet
of summer's end. In time's maze
over the fall fields, we name names
that went west from here, names
that rest on graves. We open
a persimmon seed to find the tree
that stands in promise,
pale, in the seed's marrow.
Geese appear high over us,
pass, and the sky closes. Abandon,
as in love or sleep, holds
them to their way, clear,
in the ancient faith: what we need
is here. And we pray, not
for new earth or heaven, but to be
quiet in heart, and in eye
clear. What we need is here.

THE PEACE OF WILD THINGS

When despair for the world grows in me
and I wake in the night at the least sound
in fear of what my life and my children's lives may be,
I go and lie down where the wood drake
rests in his beauty on the water, and the great heron feeds.
I come into the peace of wild things
who do not tax their lives with forethought
of grief. I come into the presence of still water.
And I feel above me the day-blind stars
waiting with their light. For a time
I rest in the grace of the world, and am free.

It is the destruction of the world
in our own lives that drives us
half insane, and more than half.
To destroy that which we were given
in trust: how will we bear it?
It is our own bodies that we give
to be broken, our bodies
existing before and after us
in clod and cloud, worm and tree,
that we, driving or driven, despise
in our greed to live, our haste
to die. To have lost, wantonly,
the ancient forests, the vast grasslands
is our madness, the presence
in our very bodies of our grief.

I know for a while again
the health of self-forgetfulness,
looking out at the sky through
a notch in the valley side,
the black woods wintry on
the hills, small clouds at sunset
passing across. And I know
that this is one of the thresholds
between Earth and Heaven,
from which even I may step
forth from my self and be free.

Ask the world to reveal its quietude—
not the silence of machines when they are still,
but the true quiet by which birdsongs,
trees, bellworts, snails, clouds, storms
become what they are, and are nothing else.

The best reward in going to the woods
Is being lost to other people, and
Lost sometimes to myself. I'm at the end
Of no bespeaking wire to spoil my goods;

I send no letter back I do not bring.
Whoever wants me now must hunt me down
Like something wild, and wild is anything
Beyond the reach of purpose not its own.

Wild is anything that's not at home
In something else's place. This good white oak
Is not an orchard tree, is unbespoke,
And it can live here by its will alone,

Lost to all other wills but Heaven's—wild.
So where I most am found I'm lost to you,
Presuming friend, and only can be called
Or answered by a certain one, or two.

(Sunday, July 4)

Hail to the forest born again,
that by neglect, the American benevolence,
has returned to semi-virginity, graceful
in the putrid air, the corrosive rain,
the ash-fall of Heaven-invading fire—
our time's genius to mine the light
of the world's ancient buried days
to make it poisonous in the air.
Light and greed together make a smudge
that stifles and blinds. But here
the light of Heaven's sun descends,
stained and mingled with its forms,
heavy trunk and limb, light leaf and wing,
that we must pray for clarity to see,
not raw sources, symbols, worded powers,
but fellow presences, independent, called
out of nothing by no word of ours,
blessèd, here with us.

Here where the dark-sourced stream brims up,
Reflecting daylight, making sound
In its stepped fall from cup to cup
Of tumbled rocks, singing its round

From cloud to sea to cloud, I climb
The deer road through the leafless trees
Under a wind that batters limb
On limb, still roaring as it has

Two nights and days, cold in slow spring.
But ancient song in a wild throat
Recalls itself and starts to sing
In storm-cleared light; and the bloodroot,

Twinleaf, and rue anemone
Among bare shadows rise, keep faith
With what they have been and will be
Again: frail stem and leaf, mere breath

Of white and starry bloom, each form
Recalling itself to its place
And time. Give thanks, for no windstorm
Or human wrong has altered this,

The forfeit Garden that recalls
Itself here, where both we and it

Belong; no act or thought rebels
In this brief Sabbath now, time fit

To be eternal. Such a bliss
Of bloom's no ornament, but root
And light, a saving loveliness,
Starred firmament here underfoot.

The year relents, and free
Of work, I climb again
To where the old trees wait,
Time out of mind. I hear
Traffic down on the road,
Engines high overhead.
And then a quiet comes,
A cleft in time, silence
Of metal moved by fire;
The air holds little voices,
Titmice and chickadees,
Feeding through the treetops
Among the new small leaves,
Calling again to mind
The grace of circumstance,
Sabbath economy
In which all thought is song,
All labor is a dance.
The world is made at rest,
In ease of gravity.
I hear the ancient theme
In low world-shaping song
Sung by the falling stream.
Here where a rotting log
Has slowed the flow: a shelf
Of dark soil, level laid
Above the tumbled stone.
Roots fasten it in place.

It will be here a while;
What holds it here decays.
A richness from above,
Brought down, is held, and holds
A little while in flow.
Stem and leaf grow from it.
At cost of death, it has
A life. Thus falling founds,
Unmaking makes the world.

Roberta Hill Whiteman

FROM THE SUN ITSELF

While something hummed along the river,
I sat on a wooded hill in Spring,
playing my flute to fluttering green.
At my feet, a bellwort and a fern.

A white pine churned above me.
From the sun itself, the bellwort's flame.
An oak branch snapped, then crashed behind me,
as he came through the canopy.

A huge hawk folded, fell, then opening
his mantle, swooped under oaks with no qualm.
With the mastery of ashes, he twisted, lifted
and turned, breezing easily on broad wings.

I clung to a high note, more for my health
than his. No stranger to the scheming wind,
he hit the rim of the hill, flicked
his red tail and broke into blue.

The mottled light underneath his wings
scattered into beeches below.
Heady with flight, I stood silent, for
he knew what the human heart renounces.

He circled east and flew to the sun itself.
So drawn to him by my longing,
I didn't hear the deepening drone.
As bellwort, fern and pine bough grew greener,

the chopper's keen blade lagged for a moment,
after a dawn raid on the gypsy moths.
The pilot may never know he was swinging
the fierce edge of our twilight.

UNDERGROUND WATER

When spirit is heavy, it turns to water . . .
                              CARL JUNG

A child, awaking, takes the long way home.
Rain glistens on the window.
He hears voices abandoning weather. Narrow streams
trickle in the dark between streetlights
and a cloud folds down like a rag.
Down gutters, a dark field waits his escape.
There, birds flutter in the wet leaves
while clover blooms like the only stars.
A smell of mud skims through the room,
tired perfume on a blush of air.
A cat in heat asks its question
and tap water thumps its way alone.
As he walks by, the dresser creaks
and swirls of paint sigh like night blooming dahlias.
Cabbage moths dancing against his chin,
he pads to his parents' bed and crawls between them.
The sound of underground water rustles
like taffeta around their hips. It pulls him
toward the warmth of sea plums.
A birthmark of foam encircles his neck.
Listening in the quilted dark,
he slips away to another sun. From there,
he watches mother stare at a smoky bulb

in this last room. She'll never hear
the lilies rise, the weeds spin in the shallows
or water lap the half-awakened stones.
She hasn't words enough to lock his days.
They say goodbye on every heartbeat.
At every moment, dozens of waterbirds
whir in flight, their quicksilver wings
confusing the leaves. Goodbye,
goodbye, the curtains breathe,
while memories, those stains on linen, remain
the last design. With bones of moonlight,
she skirts the water's edge. On her head,
a cap of fluttering voices. Cabbage moths,
her mad soul's journeymen, play in her hair.
Turning in her sleep, she feels again his breath
upon her cheek. Softer than the eye closing in death,
a curled leaf falls from his forehead
and is lost in the grass.

Charles Wright

WAITING FOR TU FU

Snip, snip goes wind through the autumn trees.
I move my bed to the battlefront,
                              dead leaves like a blanket of moth bodies
Up to the necks of the cold grasses.
It crunches like pecan shells underfoot.
It crinks my back where I lie
                              gazing into the beaten artifice
Of gold leaf and sky.

How vast the clouds are, how vast as they troll and pass by.
Splendid and once-removed, like lives, they never come back.
Does anyone think of them?
Everything's golden from where I lie.
                              Even the void
Beyond the void the clouds cross.
Even the knowledge that everything's fire,
                              and nothing ever comes back.

All that was yesterday, or last week,
Or somebody else's line of talk
                              Words rise like mist from my body,
Prayer-smoke, a snowy comfort.
The Greek-thin hammered gold artifacts
                              and glazed inlay
Of landscape and sky
Accept it as incense, for they are used to such things.

What have you done with your life,
                                    you've asked me, as you've asked yourself,
What has it come to,
Carrying us like a barge toward the century's end
And sheer drop-off into millennial history?
I remember an organ chord one Sunday in North Carolina.
I remember the smell of white pines,
                                    Vitalis and lye soap.

O we were pure and holy in those days,
The August sunlight candescing our short-sleeved shirt fronts,
The music making us otherwise.
O we were abstract and true.
How could we know that grace would fall from us like shed skin,
That reality, our piebald dog, would hunt us down?

The seasons reshuffle and set me.
Cattle as large as clouds
                        lumber across my mind's sky
And children rise in the wind
Like angels over the lake, sad cataracted eye—

I remember cutting its surface once in a green canoe,
Eye that saw everything, that now sees nothing at all . . .

Where is my life going in these isolate outlands,
You questioned once in a verse.

I ask the same thing,
                    wreckage of broken clouds too far to count,
The landscape, like God, a circle whose center is everywhere
And circumference nowhere,
Dead end of autumn, everything caught between stone-drift and
        stone.

Black winter bird flocks side-wheel
From tree lung to grief-empty tree lung,
                              lawn furniture
Imprints, unsat in. It's late.
Darkness, black phosphorus, smokes forth in the peaches and white
        pines.
The pile driver footing the new bridge
Cuts off, the bird flocks cough up and out.

I've read *Reflections in Autumn,*
        I've been through the Three Gorges, I've done Chengdu . . .
Much easier here to find you out,
A landscape yourself by now,
Canebrake and waterbrake, inviolable in the memory.
Immortals, you once said, set forth again in their boats.
White hair, white hair. Drift away.

ALL LANDSCAPE IS ABSTRACT, AND TENDS
TO REPEAT ITSELF

I came to my senses with a pencil in my hand
And a piece of paper in front of me.
                                     To the years
Before the pencil, O, I was the resurrection.
Still, who knows where the soul goes,
Up or down,
                    after the light switch is turned off, who knows?

It's late August, and prophets are calling their bears in.

The sacred is frightening to the astral body,
As is its absence.
                    We have to choose which fear is our consolation.
Everything comes *ex alto,*
We'd like to believe, the origin and the end, or
Non-origin and the non-end,
                              each distant and inaccessible.

Over the Blue Ridge, the whisperer starts to whisper in tongues.

Remembered landscapes are left in me
The way a bee leaves its sting,
                              hopelessly, passion-placed,
Untranslatable language.

Non-mystical, insoluble in blood, they act as an opposite
To the absolute, whose words are a solitude, and set to music.

All forms of landscape are autobiographical.

WATCHING THE EQUINOX ARRIVE IN
CHARLOTTESVILLE, SEPTEMBER 1992

2:23 p.m.
                    The season glides to a click.
Nobody says a word
From where I sit, shadows dark flags from nothing's country,
Birds in the deep sky, then not,
Cricket caught in the outback between a grass spear and a leaf.
The quince bush
Is losing its leaves in the fall's early chemotherapy,
And stick-stemmed spikes of the lemon tree
Spink in the sun.
Autumnal outtakes, autumnal stills . . .

Mockingbird, sing me a song.
Back here, where the windfall apples rot to the bee's joy,
Where the peach sheaths and pear sheaths piebald and brindle,
Where each year the orchard unlearns
                                    everything it's been taught,
The weekend's rainfall
Pools its untroubled waters,
Doves putter about in the still-green limbs of the trees,
Ants inch up the cinder blocks and lawn spiders swing from
        the vines.
You've got to learn to unlearn things, the season repeats.
For every change there's a form.

———

Open your mouth, you are lost, close your mouth, you are lost,
So the Buddhists say.
                        They also say,
Live in the world unattached to the dust of the world.

Not so easy to do when the thin, monotonous tick of the universe
Painfully pries our lips apart,
                           and dirties our tongues
With soiled, incessant music.
Not so easy to do when the right front tire blows out,
Or the phone rings at 3 a.m.
                   and the ghost-voice says, "It's 911, please hold."
They say, enter the blackness, the form of forms. They say,
No matter how we see ourselves, sleeping and dreaming see us
       as light.

Still, there's another story,
                     that what's inside us is what's outside us:
That what we see outside ourselves we'll soon see inside ourselves.
It's visible, and is our garment.
Better, perhaps, to wear that.
Better to live as though we already lived the afterlife,
Unattached to our cape of starred flesh.
But Jesus said,
                Lift up the stone and you will find me,
Break open a piece of wood, I'm there.
It's hard to argue with that,

Hard to imagine a paradise beyond what the hand breaks.

———

For every force there's a change.
Mouthful of silence, mouthful of air,
                                    sing me your tune.
The wind leaves nothing alone.
How many times can summer turn to fall in one life?
Well you might ask, my old friend,
Wind-rider, wind-spirit, seeking my blood out,
                                    humming my name.

Hard work, this business of solitude.
Hard work and no gain,
Mouthful of silence, mouthful of air.
Everything's more than it seems back here. Everything's less.

Like migrating birds, our own lives drift away from us.
How small they become in the blank sky, how colorful,
On their way to wherever they please.
We keep our eyes on the ground,
                                on the wasp and pinch bug,
As the years grind by and the seasons churn, north and south.
We keep our eyes on the dirt.
Under the limp fins of the lemon tree, we inhabit our absence.
Crows cross-hatch and settle in,
                                red birds and dust sparrows
Spindle and dart through the undergrowth.
We don't move. We watch, but we don't move.

WHY, IT'S AS PRETTY AS A PICTURE

A shallow thinker, I'm tuned
                         to the music of things,
The conversation of birds in the dusk-damaged trees,
The just-cut grass in its chalky moans,
The disputations of dogs, night traffic, I'm all ears
To all this and half again.

And so I like it out here,
Late spring, off-colors but firming up, at ease among half things.
At ease because there is no overwhelming design
                                I'm sad heir to,
At ease because the dark music of what surrounds me
Plays to my misconceptions, and pricks me, and plays on.

It is a kind of believing without belief that we believe in,
This landscape that goes
                        no deeper than the eye, and poises like
A postcard in front of us
As though we'd settled it there, just so,
Halfway between the mind's eye and the mind, just halfway

And yet we tend to think of it otherwise. Tonight,
For instance, the wind and the mountains and half-moon talk
Of unfamiliar things in a low familiar voice,
As though their words, however small, were putting the world
       in place.

And they are, they are,
                        the place inside the place inside the place.

The postcard's just how we see it, and not how it is.
Behind the eye's the other eye,
                        and the other ear.
The moonlight whispers in it, the mountains imprint upon it,
Our eyelids close over it,
Dawn and the sunset radiate from it like Eden.

Mary Oliver

THE SUMMER DAY

Who made the world?
Who made the swan, and the black bear?
Who made the grasshopper?
This grasshopper, I mean—
the one who has flung herself out of the grass,
the one who is eating sugar out of my hand,
who is moving her jaws back and forth instead of up and down—
who is gazing around with her enormous and complicated eyes.
Now she lifts her pale forearms and thoroughly washes her face.
Now she snaps her wings open, and floats away.
I don't know exactly what a prayer is.
I do know how to pay attention, how to fall down
into the grass, how to kneel down in the grass,
how to be idle and blessed, how to stroll through the fields,
which is what I have been doing all day.
Tell me, what else should I have done?
Doesn't everything die at last, and too soon?
Tell me, what is it you plan to do
with your one wild and precious life?

SLEEPING IN THE FOREST

I thought the earth
remembered me, she
took me back so tenderly, arranging
her dark skirts, her pockets
full of lichens and seeds. I slept
as never before, a stone
on the riverbed, nothing
between me and the white fire of the stars
but my thoughts, and they floated
light as moths among the branches
of the perfect trees. All night
I heard the small kingdoms breathing
around me, the insects, and the birds
who do their work in the darkness. All night
I rose and fell, as if in water, grappling
with a luminous doom. By morning
I had vanished at least a dozen times
into something better.

THE OLD POETS OF CHINA

Wherever I am, the world comes after me.
It offers me its busyness. It does not believe
that I do not want it. Now I understand
why the old poets of China went so far and high
into the mountains, then crept into the pale mist.

Alvin Aubert

BAPTISM

ancestral pearls so deep, so blue
blue oozes from a teeming swamp.
a river rolls its ancient silt gulfward.
a muddy voice rises. 'come here pretty
baby, come sit down on my cypress knee.
run your willowy fingers thru the speckled moss
of my oaken heart. jordan river so chilly
and cold, religion so sweet.' mary mary
mother of sweet hallelujahs, make way
for this wild explosion of jubilant
white-robed sisters settled to their feast
of succulent crabs and bisque.
you miracle-motored scooters along
inaccessible ways, intrepid seekers of depths,
bring back that summer breeze that soulful
drummer breeze. stir this simmering black
pot to a cauldron of fructifying memory.
swirl this stagnant blood, this cold
streaming liquid pearl. trouble
this rooted tongue . . .
were you there when the preacher he dunked
sweet hannah deep down the western bank
and she rose white-robe-clinging wet
out of pearly blue blaze?—go down,
sweet hannah! run, river: trouble my song.
were you on the set when black king

of the blues-fiery throat traded in
his box for a travelin piano?—made
the levee his road, the sure way of
the river?—willow his tent, rock his
pillow, cold cold ground his bed?—
were you there? if you saw the sun
lay its thousand daily kisses the breadth
of that muddy bosom, felt the river bed
rock in the cradle of its mighty run
and the cypress swamp turn its oozing
blues to gold in the deep of midnight,
you were there. saw blue and coal
black king saw him sing. heard his
deep timbre entwine with another
sweet as rose water and old as wine.
black magnolia of the valley, queen
of the gold scissors. cleanest
belly button maker this side eden.
king singing from the midnight coal
black and blueness of his lonesome
road, his sad/happy song swaddling the wail
at the pearly root of this lifelicking tongue.

NAT TURNER IN THE CLEARING

Ashes, Lord—
But warm still from the fire that cheered us,
Lighted us in this clearing where it seems
Scarcely an hour ago we feasted on
Burnt pig from our tormentor's unwilling
Bounty and charted the high purpose your
Word had launched us on. And now, my comrades
Dead, or taken; your servant, pressed by the
Bloody yelps of hounds, forsaken, save for
The stillness of the word that persists quivering
And breath-moist on his tongue: and these faint coals
Soon to be rushed to dying glow by the
Indifferent winds of miscarriage—What now,
My Lord? A priestess once, they say, could write
On leaves, unlock the time-bound spell of deeds
Undone. I let fall upon these pale remains
Your breath-moist word, preempt the winds, and give
Them now their one last glow, that some dark child
In time to come might pass this way and, in
This clearing, read and know.

James Baker Hall

WELCOMING THE SEASON'S FIRST INSECTS

Each with its own language, contingencies,
catalogues, instructions. When I imagine
all the creatures living within me,
within one cell of me,

I become a sun. All the midges
hanging over all the meadows

swarm within me, becoming one sound.
I sit here like a wishbone
in the garden's late light,

early spring, the sun's
tuning fork. The ants

ornament my skin in a line. Small
by reason of the great distance
between them and my eye

they carry me off. The weight
of their feet

sings, bless us,
we've made it
this far.

KNEELING AT EASTER TO THE SEASON'S FIRST BLOODROOT

for Cia White

Eventually one spring enough ground was turned,
a windstorm occurred at the right moment,

the rest we piece together. Even if a human
had been here he could not have seen
what was rising
from the earth

and traveling by cloud east southeast over two ridges,
to a large stagnant pond—
owned by a man named Connors—

nor could anyone have seen it reappear,
out of the rain, as algae.
No one was here

when the grasses first appeared, or the whales.
No one was here long before that, the sun
circled and drilled, sparks leaped,
a bolt of lightning forked,
the earth was cooling,
one cell became two.

THE BUFFALO

crossing the yard to the old wall
I'm drawn along a circle
through each thing a full moon
seen over a considerable area of the earth
including the vast oceans rises
and walks down the wall
and through me
in the evolving white shape of a cat
for years these stones lay afield
gathering his footsteps even the clicks
sound old and have come a long way
his fur slipping through my hands
what did my ancestor hear
upon seeing the Shawnee step into
this moonlight with a small stone taken up
and shaped to his use what did the Shawnee hear
when the gun was cocked where did the sounds go
when the buffalo were slaughtered
were they fixed in time
or were they freed
into the real world mistaken
for snapping twigs or distant
thunder or history at night
when the small creatures walk this wall
isn't it the same gravity audible
the weight of each thing settling

defining the size of its earth the dead
clicking along in the moonlight with us
great silences in between
and within each of them
and dwindling herds

Gladys Cardiff

WHERE FIRE BURNS

I.

Where fire burns in the hollow sycamore,
　　　smoke like a vague feather lifting
　　　up from the island,
　　　and the world is cold,
　　　where all the animals wait
　　　on the river's edge
　　　while Water Spider weaves
　　　a *tusti* bowl, and steals
　　　across the waves,
　　　where in the little crucible
　　　she carries on her back
　　　an orange piece of the Thunder's gift,
　　　there all the fires
　　　of hearth and harvest,
　　　the conflagrations to come,
　　　the everlasting fire of the sacred mounds,
　　　leap into being.

II.

Where fire burns in the Carolinas
　　　sweeping up the hillsides
　　　in a red and gold combustion
　　　of blossoming azaleas,

and blue smoke rises above
immovable mountains,
and it is 1898,
sixty years after Going Snake
heard peal after peal of thunder
on a cloudless day of departure,
you Suate, implacable, a Chosen One,
will speak to Sundays's congregation
of Wasi and God's voice
in a burning bush,
and tell stories
while the man from Washington
writes in his book
"The rabbit was the leader of them all
in mischief."

III.

Where the fires of generation have brought me here
    to the opposite end of the land,
    to work late at night
    while my husband and children sleep,
    where out from the yellow pages
    the tongues of fire ignite
    and wily rabbit dances
    into the broom-grass
    tricking the wolf again,
    it is like gathering nuts
    after the leaf-burning, stirring and sifting

through ashes and husks,
cracking the vowels and consonants
of a language I need to know,
trying to get the taste of them.
Because of our son
with hair blacker than soot,
and eyes that become darker every year
and more impenetrable,
for our daughter with hair as orange
as fire on the hill,
her eyes the color of smoke,
I gather the names and places,
these nutmeats sweetened
with the char of fire,
that they may hold
wherever they go
inextinguishable seeds,
words that say
tsita'ga, "I am standing,"
da nita'ga, "They are standing
together as one."

Richard Taylor

DREAMING THE BUFFALO BACK

In droves their swollen humps
rise from the shallows, hooves
nicking the asphalt with tiny moons.

Tracking the scent of salt,
they graze resolutely east,
past patios, through fences
and staked tomatoes
toward Stamping Ground,
the bowl-shaped wallow
where they will hunker and swill.

Muzzle to tail, they migrate.
To Sulphur Lick and Great Crossing,
to all the places that carry
their lost names. Shaggy pilgrims,
bearded, robed in snow,
they bunch at night
to blanket their quaking calves.

Under a spatterwork of stars
they herd in the lush pasturage
of dream. Without predators,
they reclaim the landscape
encompassed between the parentheses
of their upturned horns.

Loosed from memory,
they cannot even dream
the space where we might be.

INVENTORYING WILDFLOWERS ALONG GRINDSTONE CREEK ON DERBY DAY

for Marshall Thompson

Noodling down the steep ridge,
crossing and recrossing
the dribbly branch
past overhangs and platters
of upturned stone, we list
twenty-nine species in bloom.
Up to our knees in may-apples,
we step gingerly over
the larkspur's florets,
over the fragile nodes
of shooting star, bloodroot
nodding in the half-formed shade.

At the bottom of the ravine
where branch meets creek,
tiers of wild hyacinth rising
pale blue along the slopes,
the waters fills our ears
with a purling clarity that cleanses
all imperfection, all signs
to implicate us in our century.

Here, not much bigger than a breadloaf,
letters chiselled out in tiny canyons,
inches from a sprouting buckeye,
we find the marble headstone:

'Kate Willow Thompson
1974 Springtime'

Bloodroot, crib death, springtime.

PREMISES

What we're looking for
is a place
with none of the conveniences,
where the rocks
have not trimmed their nails.

Our needs are few.
Some bedrock, some water,
a view of the moon:
tadpoles swim in the print
of one hoof.

What we don't find
we'll scavenge and build.
We'll bring our own tools
and plant by the signs.

All we are asking is
a goldfinch in the chicory.

Jane Kenyon

FEBRUARY: THINKING OF FLOWERS

Now wind torments the field,
turning the white surface back
on itself, back and back on itself,
like an animal licking a wound.

Nothing but white—the air, the light;
only one brown milkweed pod
bobbing in the gully, smallest
brown boat on the immense tide.

A single green sprouting thing
would restore me. . . .

Then think of the tall delphinium,
swaying, or the bee when it comes
to the tongue of the burgundy lily.

WITH THE DOG AT SUNRISE

Although we always come this way
I never noticed before that the poplars
growing along the ravine
shine pink in the light of winter dawn.

What am I going to say
in my letter to Sarah—a widow
at thirty-one, alone in the violence
of her grief, sleepless,
and utterly cast down?

I look at the lithe, pink trees more carefully,
remembering Stephen, the photographer.
With the hunger of two I take them in.
Perhaps I can tell her that.

The dog furrows his brow while pissing long
and thoughtfully against an ancient hemlock.
The snow turns the saffron of a monk's robe
and acrid steam ascends.

Searching for God is the first thing and the last,
but in between such trouble, and such pain.

Far up in the woods where no one goes
deer take their ease under the great
pines, nose to steaming nose. . . .

Jim Wayne Miller

GOING TO SLEEP BY A TROUTSTREAM

From where he lay the steady crash of water
down over rocks
a hundred yards upstream
was no more than the far-off waterfall
a sudden wind set roaring in the treetops.

Like icy water running from a bold spring
that wind came pouring off a thunderstorm
back on the headwaters.
He lay like a trout
hugging the bottom of its flowing.

Over his head, toward the surface of that windstream,
willow leaves, silver in the flow,
became schooled minnows going against the current.
He saw them swimming, swimming in one place;

then, letting go, he drifted
backwards in the flow
and came to rest
where the light of stars grew down
like bonewhite roots
under a bank of wet leaves, rotten wood,
darkness.

SHAPES

When he saw people flowing out of the mountains,
leaving like a line of clanking coalcars,
his life grew damp and heavy in his flesh,
turned dark and cold
as charred wood in a rained-out fire.

The smallest thing, though, still could fire his spirit—
a chopping ax far off in the woods,
foxhounds running on the ridge at night,
the cries of children playing in the creek,
a dog lapping water in the dark.

When he found deer tracks on the logging roads
his life grew light and dry.
Near the weathered silver of old barns
his life caught fire
and he studied shapes in the flame of his own spirit.

WINTER DAYS

He loved warm winter days when woodlands opened
their summer secrets to a passerby.
Treeshadows lay crisscrossed, low creeks deepened,
borrowing their cold blue from the sky.

Icicles glistened on the rock-backed ridges,
a field of broomsage hissed in the wind.
Frost and fencepost shadows melted by edges
of pasture-fields where coal-black cattle stood.

Sunlight ricocheted from tin-topped barns,
streaking the chalk walls of the limestone quarry.
Between white sycamores the river turned,
sure of where it was going, in no hurry.

John Lane

THE HOMECOMING OF OSCEOLA

Edisto Island, South Carolina

Fifty miles south of Charleston,
south of the cell at Fort Moultrie
where he once dreamed the long hours
through sticky heat and silences,
I walk the last high tide of the day
to find bones of glacial South Carolina
washed up from back marshes.

I recite particulars of that gone world:
Glyptodont, mastodon, bison, dugong.
Their fragments rattle my pockets.
Wind skitters along tops of waves,
up dunes, to the estuarine glint
beyond. An incoming tide measures
marsh grass, making a low sound
like someone sighing.

                    *

From a hammock deep in *Pa-hay-okee*
he listened as flat-bottomed boats
of the U.S. Navy slid through thick
saw grass and mosquitoes.

"We will flush him like a rat
from his savage hole,"

an Army captain mumbled to a slow fire
to dry thatch-palm and torchwood,

to ten men, snake-scared and malarial,
who dreamed of Baltimore and Richmond.

They listened too,
and the Seminole War dragged on.

                    *

Ivory from the tusk of mammoth,
tooth of *Equus,* tooth of *Bison bison,*
dugong ribs, cracked leg bones of *Ursus.*

                    *

Last winter, walking here at Edisto
I dug half a skullcap from the tidal sand—
the frontal bone, eye-ridges intact.
The bleached whole of it brown
from tannin stain, buried years
under water of cypress swamps.
I placed it over my ear—
wanting a song in the dead
long months before spring—
that tight curve of bone
held a soft roar,
like a tightly cupped hand
or the dull slap of sea
on a turtle-haunted shore

or a winter wind rattling
dry palmetto fronds gathered for kindling.

*

Osceola finally rooted out, brought to
South Carolina.

Seminole, "Men-who-go-free,"
of the five tribes of the Creek, of the Piedmont
and mountains.

The guard spat in standing water,
leaned on a sweating stone wall
next to a windowless cell.

Inside, Osceola's last chant
rose from the cot, from the stoneware mug,
pried the stones with sound—
his windows to the next world.

*

I walk up the receding beach,
past peeling wood rails of empty cottages,
through low thick brush and live oak
to reach the back of the island,
where St. Pierre Creek eats
at the Indian mound.

*

The guard listened:

spittle spread on the water,
a soul reentering a body.

*

A mound of midden
arches flat coastal country.
It would take twenty years to grub
this many shell fish from the tidal creeks.
I still smell the oysters and clams steaming
in salt and fresh oak, or eaten raw
and piled here 4,000 years ago.
A lone buck is spooked
in dry leaves by my hard boots.
I look out over a marsh the color of shale.
It is that moment just before the tide
shifts, or right after.
The empty shells hiss.

*

"And you who keep me here
know nothing about cages."

The coast is quiet.
A creek turns over in its sleep.

THE RIVER FALLING

Once, we slept in oak woods,
zipped our two bags together, pulled free
of flannel shirts, shucked jeans,
counted the sad light of planes
flying to Asheville until the darkness
of dying oak leaves offered up some light.
All night Bradley Falls argued the moon down.

That morning, we climbed down,
took off our clothes, listened
to a song of water leveling with stone.
You sat in a hole where the river once
licked its own bed. I squatted, pressed silt
in my palms, caught round stones dragging
the creek bottom. The fall sun was up,
cliff-high, a star in a stub oak.

I squinted, spoke,
"You know I could be this river, easily
live my life between two places, two women."

You watched the falls, the perfect sadness
of the river falling. I swear the wet air
hummed, water dug for something to hold.
Then you turned, said,
"Then go, the seed's in us all, this leaving."

David Budbill (Judevine Mountain)

ALWAYS IN THESE ANCIENT CHINESE PAINTINGS

Always in these Chinese paintings, the rocks, the sky, the fog,
       the endless mountains loom
              over the tiny humans

down there fishing in those boats upon that peaceful river
       down there in the lower right-hand corner, or
              there they barely are

climbing up that narrow mountain path, up and up, fading into
       those remote and towering mountains
              way over on the left,

and always, always you have to look and look before you find
       the little people lost as they are
              in mist and distance,

in that expanse of rock, sky, trees, of mountains and rivers
       without end, and always you can barely see them, which,
              of course, is as it should be.

SUCH SELF-INDULGENCE AND SLOTH!

All morning I sit at my desk drinking tea,
reading ancient poets,
and writing my own ridiculous poems.

In the afternoon I go wandering through the woods
to see wildflowers and listen to birds
and the wind singing through the trees.

Then I sit beside the brook down in the bottom
of the ravine where the rock outcroppings loom
over my head, and I listen to the waterfall.

Such self-indulgence and sloth make me so happy!
I wonder who will pay me to be useless and in love.

WHAT ISSA HEARD

Two hundred years ago Issa heard the morning birds
singing sutras to this suffering world.

I heard them too, this morning, which must mean,

since we will always have a suffering world,
we must also always have a song.

QUOTING T'AO CH'IEN

A thousand years may be beyond me
but I can turn this morning into forever.

For thirty years I've studied ancient-Chinese poets
and Taoist texts, and often I have longed to abjure
this world, these days, to see through the red dust
of our fleeting lives and thus accede to immortality.

But, alas and luckily, for me—*character is fate.*
I love this world too much to want to find a way
away from it. I give my soul to my senses.

I love the sound of birds, the sight of wind
passing through the trees, the swollen cock,
the soaking vulva, a bowl of vegetables and noodles,
a cup of wine, the sweet aroma of some tea.

How could heaven be anywhere but here?
This place, now, today . . . is eternity,
and it is here in me and in my dying life.

Thorpe Moeckel

BARTRAM'S TRAIL

To follow Bartram's trail upstream, past Tugaloo,
to cross the Chattooga River at Earl's Ford,
to go up the Warwoman Valley,
up past the cascades & bridalveils of Finney Creek,
up along the Continental Divide
between Rabun Bald & Hickory Knob,
is to crawl, is to hopscotch
between the doghobble and the yellowroot,
the rhododendron and the laurel, hand over hand,
inch by dirty, glistening inch;
to follow Bartram is to squirm, prostrate,
under the lattice-work of limb,
the umbrellaed variations of lanceolate,
the way the lungless slip like tongues
through the tiny, moss-flamed grottoes,
oblivious to four-legged jesuses
walking on the water's white-lit roostertails;
to follow Bartram's trail is to go
wet-socked, knee-weary & briar-inked,
is to limbo under shadows
mosaiced and three-quarter domed;
to follow Bartram as far as the end
is split, past the leastmost echo,
past the hiccup of wild mint and galax,
the azalea, the teaberry, the trailing arbutus;

to follow Bartram into the shade of the giant poplar,
across the intersection of trunk and root,
across the blighted chestnuts,
is to find the place
where no pattern goes unrepeated,
the place where the first ashes were spread.

FERN

Carboniferous one, coal's secret agent—
your fruit dot is in the cirrus today,
and though I'm trying to live like that,
multitudinous, wired to send roots, connect,
I know you used to be massive, tree-sized,
and would have feared seeing you then—
Paleozoic skyscraper—standing in your shade,
unable to blot you out with a step,
the way I do walking these drainages & slopes,
worrying your particular names,
cinnamon, ostrich, maidenhair—
because you don't flower, you don't flower—
how they're entwined & bring me closer
to your center, that slipperyness: earned grace.

BOLIN CREEK

I think of the bream in your red clay shallows,
their olive-hued longitudes
and copper breasts, their
huge pupils & the way
they squiggle,
like thoughts, or desire, nowhere
according to nothing
determinable;
I think of their silence,
how mushroom clouds of silt rise
where they brush rock or limb;

and of your undercut banks, how, along them,
amongst sphagnum and spleenwort,
several trees rise from one
system of roots, at
the sun's favorite angle;

of the wild ginger
along the root-studded footpath,
the cedar, umbrella magnolia,
gifts of the sycamore;

the rhombozoids & parallelograms of bedrock,
and how, in June, in the stagnant runs, as if
the eye contained all the heart

did & did not know about love,
there's the bottom
of one hundred leaves to look at,
ironwood leaves, reflected
in a chain-link configuration, top lit
& unctuous like
accidental filigree—I think of that,
and of the cicada's trill crescendos
in the brain-dead afternoons, and the dogwalkers
conversing, and the sound
of mountain bikes—squeal of brake pad on rim—
coming through the hardwoods and the pines.

ON BEING EATEN

The curt savagery
                of her paw
        plows my spine. I hear
a magpie; it sounds
                        too neutral. On my knees
                        there's a stone,
            I chunk it, hoping
to meet skull, & hard enough,
                                but there's a light
        so bright I know
it's over. I know without
                        having to be told.
            I won't be told,
because I'm lupine, because
        she's found
the omelet
                & is rubbing her neck
in my guts
        as if perfume. Know this:
                        there's ecstasy
                in death, and some days in moans
your name,
                it claws & it moans.

Davis McCombs

PONDS

The night we lost thirteen of them,
tremors shook along New Madrid fault.
In field after field the moon rose
to its own face echoed back,
cattle circling a crater's rim.
Along these margins, life had fixed—
an algal bloom, its underwater thud.
They were sucked through vast caverns.
In the Caveland, every pond's a fluke.
Let them be brief, then, as the land
gives up the ghost of fog, morning
in the sway-backed enclaves.
Already the clay dries and separates
along small faults. We expect no return.
Not even a tadpole's kink in mud
where Jesus bugs made miracles
the only way they could—
as if there were no underworld,
as if the pond would last.

FLOWSTONE

How the water behaves
determines their shape and composition:
stalactites, a rimstone dam.
Above, great fossil slabs
slough off in geologic time,
limestone leached and percolating
into caverns. At a cubic inch
per century, this is cave-making
in reverse. But to what end?
A caver pushing virgin passage
out beyond the sandstone lip
emerges into verticals, hung
and glinting where his carbide falls.
Is it for this or the process?
What an ancient sea set down in even lines
is worked into a cursive scrawl,
as run-off through the bedding planes
recalls
a steamy day, an inland sea,
the continent adrift—
south of the equator but bearing north.

THE RIVER AND UNDER THE RIVER

At dusk every day, our cattle leave the river,
single-file, trundling their weight to the upper pastures.
And every night, the river is left to itself, infertile
and self-loathing, most beautiful when it comes close
to absence; its grooves and grottoes hum
with the noise of a landscape's slow consumption.
If I put my ear to the ground
could I hear the drag of the river turning
limestone into silt? Would it tell of Carlos pulled
through water on a slim and muscly night at Turnhole Bend?
I want to know the missing part of his story
that ends with the flush of foxfire on a grave—
as if from the body's heat fading out.
Tonight the river is at work dissolving, solving
over and over the riddle of its loosening.
I want to know how to hear it, and what it might teach me:
how to inhabit this thing of bone, gut, and blood,
this part of me that would not vanish if I vanished.

ACKNOWLEDGMENTS

I would like to thank Laura Sutton, John Lane, John Elder, and John Tallmadge for their suggestions and editorial assistance in shaping *Field Work.*

Biographical information for the poets included in *Field Work* has been culled from: *Mountain Home: The Wilderness Poetry of Ancient China,* selected and translated by David Hinton; the Academy of American Poets Web site, www.poets.org; the Native American Authors Project; the *Harper's Anthology of 20th Century Native American Poetry,* edited by Duane Niatum; and *Modern Poems,* edited by Richard Ellmann and Robert O'Clair.

AUTHOR BIOGRAPHIES

ROBERT FROST (1874–1963) is the father of all modern American poets working in the naturalist tradition, particularly poets living in the eastern United States. Frost lived for many years on a farm in New Hampshire and much of his work is associated with that rugged landscape. At John F. Kennedy's request, Frost read a poem during the 1961 presidential inauguration.

LI PO (701–762) spent most of his life wandering through China, drinking in taverns, and occasionally serving as a court poet. He deplored convention and wrote wine-inspired poems known as "wildgrass calligraphy." In life and in art, Li Po practiced the selfless spontaneity known as *wu-wei*. According to translator David Hinton, this means that "to live as part of the earth's process of change is to live one's most authentic self." Late in life, Li Po found himself on the losing side of a civil war and he spent his final years in exile.

TU FU (712–770) If Li Po represented the amoral, Taoist side of Chinese thought, Tu Fu stood for the socially engaged philosophy of Confucius. Civil war broke out in China when Tu Fu was forty-four, and he spent the rest of his life moving his family away from the fighting and brooding over the collapse of a great dynasty. As translator David Hinton has suggested, Tu Fu's philosophy can be distilled into one line from his poetry: "The nation falls into ruins; rivers and mountains continue."

WANG WEI (701–761) was a revered landscape painter and musician as well as a poet. He spent his career as a government bureaucrat, but still escaped to a mountain retreat on the Wheel-Rim River to paint and compose. A follower of Zen Buddhism, he wrote poems in which the poet's inner mindscape merged with the outer landscape in such a way that the ego dissolves and the mind becomes a reflection of the world's "ten thousand things."

HAN SHAN (COLD MOUNTAIN) (c. 7th–9th centuries) lived in the Heaven Terrace Mountains of southeast China, but little is known about him outside of legend. A wild, free spirit, he roamed the mountains, writing poems on trees and rocks. A local government prefect gathered these scattered poems together in a collection that has survived and earned the admiration of Eastern and Western readers in the centuries that followed.

JAMES STILL (1906–2001) studied with Robert Penn Warren, John Crowe Ransom, and the rest of the agrarian "Fugitives" at Vanderbilt University. In 1931, he began working, for room and board only, as the librarian of the Hindman Settlement School in Eastern Kentucky. With the exception of a stint in the Air Force during World War II, he lived and worked at the Settlement School for the rest of his life. His 1940 novel *River of Earth* is one of the richest chronicles of life in the Appalachian coal fields. He was selected to read his poem "Heritage" for the 1996 PBS series *The United States of Poetry*.

JAMES WRIGHT (1927–1980) referred to his birthplace, Martins Ferry, Ohio, as the "triggering town" of many of his poems. He received a B.A. from Kenyon College and then served with the U.S. Army in Japan. Back stateside, he studied with the poet Theodore Roethke at the University of Washington. He fought a lifelong battle with the bottle that eventually ended in a draw. In 1971, his *Collected Poems* won the Pulitzer Prize.

LORINE NIEDECKER (1903–1970) spent most of her life on the remote Black Hawk Island in northern Wisconsin. She grew up poor, the daughter of a fisherman, and she herself often performed menial work to pay the bills. While employed by the WPA during the Depression, she wrote *Wisconsin: A Guide to the Badger State*. Though isolated geographically, she befriended through letters the objectivist poet Louis Zukofsky, from whom she learned her minimalist style. Since her death, *A Granite Pail: The Selected Poems of Lorine Niedecker* has garnered a larger audience. The British poet Basil Bunting called Niedecker "easily the finest female American poet."

A. R. AMMONS (1926–2001) was born in North Carolina, took a degree in science from Wake Forest University, and later became an executive in a glass-making firm. In the 1960s he began teaching at Cornell University. His *Collected Poems: 1951–1971* won the National Book Award. Ammons was known to type a whole book of poetry on one roll of adding machine paper. He wrote with a naturalist's eye as well as a poet's ear. His one-sentence poem *Garbage* won the Pulitzer Prize in 1993.

HAYDEN CARRUTH (1921–) was educated at the University of North Carolina and has spent many years living in northern Vermont. He often writes with a less-than-romantic tone about rural life and the tough men and women, his neighbors, who still live off the land. Carruth has published over thirty books. *Collected Shorter Poems, 1946–1991* won the National Book Critics' Circle Award in 2001 and *Scrambled Eggs and Whiskey* won the National Book Award in 1996.

DENISE LEVERTOV (1923–1997) was born in Essex, England, and settled in New York and Maine in the 1950s, at which time she became a naturalized citizen. Her father was a descendant of the renowned Russian rabbi Schneour Zalmon, who was reputed to understand the speech of birds. In the 1960s, Levertov was active in protesting the war in Vietnam and she served as the poetry editor of the *Nation*. She published over twenty volumes of poetry with James Laughlin's pioneering press, New Directions.

WENDELL BERRY (1934–) is a farmer, poet, novelist, polemicist, and one of the most respected conservationists in the United States. A Kentucky native, he studied writing under Wallace Stegner at Stanford, then returned to farm and write along the Kentucky River. His landmark book on agriculture, *The Unsettling of America*, remains hugely influential and even garnered the praise of Robert Redford, to which Berry is said to have responded, "Who the hell is Robert Redman?" Like William Faulkner, Berry has created an entire community in his fiction. And like many of Faulkner's characters, the people of Berry's Port William struggle to come to terms with a rapidly changing industrial world and an economy that has little room for agrarian values. His many volumes of poetry include *A Timbered Choir* and *Given*.

ROBERTA HILL WHITEMAN (1947–), a member of the Oneida Tribe, grew up near Green Bay, Wisconsin. She received an M.F.A. from the University of Montana and has taught on the Oneida and the Rosebud reservations and at the University of Wisconsin at Eau Claire. Author of *Star Quilt* and *Philadelphia Flowers*, she has worked in several states as a Poet in the Schools.

CHARLES WRIGHT (1935–) grew up in Tennessee and has spent the past few decades living in Charlottesville, Virginia. The mountains and the surrounding landscapes of central Appalachia are a continuous point of departure in Wright's poetry. He won the Pulitzer Prize for *Black Zodiac* in 1997 and the National Book Award for *Country Music* in 1983. He is the Souder Family Professor of English at the University of Virginia in Charlottesville.

MARY OLIVER (1935–) was born in Maple Heights, Ohio, and as a teenager lived briefly in the same house as Edna St. Vincent Millay. Her *New and Selected Poems* won the National Book Award and *American Primitive* won the Pulitzer Prize. She is a prolific poet whose dedication to her craft, as well as her affinity for the natural world, are both revealed in the title of a recent volume, *Why I Wake Up Early*. She lives in Provincetown, Massachusetts.

ALVIN AUBERT (1930–) is the author of six collections of poems, including *Against the Blues, If Winter Come,* and *Harlem Wrestler.* He founded the literary journal *Obsidian* and is professor emeritus at Wayne State University. Given this country's sad history of slavery and lynching, Aubert's work demonstrates why African American poets might think quite differently about the natural world than their Anglo-American counterparts.

JAMES BAKER HALL (1935–) is an accomplished art photographer and novelist as well as a poet. He taught creative writing for three decades at the University of Kentucky. He is the author of *Praeder's Letters,* a fictional correspondence in verse. His collection of selected poetry is called *The Total Light Process.*

GLADYS CARDIFF (1942–) grew up in Seattle, Washington. Her father was a member of the Owl clan of the North Carolina Cherokee, where her poem "Where Fire Burns" is set. Like James Wright, Cardiff studied with Theodore Roethke at the University of Washington. She is a member of the Native Writer's Circle of the Americas, and her poetry has appeared in many important Native American anthologies. Her most recent volume is *A Bare Unpainted Table*.

RICHARD TAYLOR (1941–) lives in Frankfort, Kentucky, where he teaches at Kentucky State University and, along with his wife Elizabeth, runs an independent bookstore called Poor Richard's. He is the author of several volumes of poetry and an experimental novel, *Girty,* about the renegade frontiersman Simon Girty. Taylor was the poet laureate of Kentucky in 1999.

JANE KENYON (1947–1995) was born in Ann Arbor, Michigan, graduated from the University of Michigan, and later moved to a New Hampshire farm with her husband, the poet Donald Hall. She published four collections of poetry during her lifetime, and *Otherwise: New and Selected Poems* was released posthumously. Kenyon also translated poems by the Russian poet Anna Akhmatova, to whose work her own poetry is often compared. She died in April 1995 after a fifteen-month battle with leukemia.

JIM WAYNE MILLER (1936–1996) was one of the leading Appalachian poets to follow in, and carry on, the lineage of James Still. His volumes of poetry include *Dialogue with a Dead Man* and *The Mountains Have Come Closer*. In the latter collection, he invented a persona, a mountain folk character called the Briar, who urges Appalachians to resist the forces of technological progress and return to an understanding of self and community that is rooted in a particular sense of place.

JOHN LANE (1954–) has taught for the last twenty years at Wofford College in his hometown of Spartanburg, South Carolina. An avid canoeist and kayaker, he mostly paddles the Chatooga River where the film *Deliverance* was made. Those experiences resulted in his book *Chatooga: Exploring the Myth of Deliverance River*. His collection of poems is called *As the World Around Us Sleeps*.

DAVID BUDBILL (1940–) was born in Ohio and lives in northern Vermont. He is the author of many books of poems, fiction, and essays, as well as eight plays. In *Moment to Moment*, the book from which Budbill's poems for this anthology are taken, Budbill adopts the persona of a poet who lives in a hermitage on Judevine Mountain and writes in the style of the ancient Chinese masters. Like the T'ang dynasty poet Cold Mountain (Han Shan), this poet goes by the name of his own mountain, Judevine.

THORPE MOECKEL (1971–) is a longtime whitewater rafter who teaches at Hollins College in Virginia. His collection *Odd Botany* won the 2000 Gerald Cable Book Award. He is also the author of *Meltlines* and *Making a Map of the River*.

DAVIS MCCOMBS (1969–) grew up in central Kentucky around Mammoth Cave, where he worked as a park ranger for a decade. He is the author of *Ultima Thule,* a collection of poems inspired by the cave, and *Dismal Rock*. He won the prestigious Yale Series of Younger Poets competition in 2000. He is currently the director of the creative writing program at the University of Arkansas.

POEM CREDITS

Ammons, A. R. "Delaware Water Gap" from *Collected Poems 1951–1971*, by A. R. Ammons, New York: Norton. Copyright © 1972 by A. R. Ammons. Used by permission of W. W. Norton & Company, Inc. "Coming Round" from *Sumerian Vistas,* by A. R. Ammons, New York: Norton. Copyright © 1987 by A. R. Ammons. Used by permission of W. W. Norton & Company, Inc. "Rapids" and "Mountain Wind" from *A Coast of Trees*, by A. R. Ammons, New York: Norton. Copyright © 1981 by A. R. Ammons. Used by permission of W. W. Norton & Company, Inc.

Aubert, Alvin. "Baptism" from *South Louisiana: New and Selected Poems,* Grosse Point Farms, Mich.: Lunchroom Press, 1985. "Nat Turner in the Clearing" from *Against the Blues,* Detroit, Mich.: Broadside Press, 1972. All poems reprinted by permission of the author.

Berry, Wendell. "The Wild Geese" and "The Peace of Wild Things" from *The Selected Poems of Wendell Berry*, Washington, D.C.: Counterpoint, 1998. Used by permission of the author. "It is the destruction of the world," "The best reward in going to the woods," "Here where the dark-sourced stream brims up," and "The year relents, and free" from *A Timbered Choir: The Sabbath Poems 1979–1997,* Washington, D.C.: Counterpoint, 1998. Used by permission of the author. "I know for a while again" and "Ask the world to reveal its quietude—" from *Given: New Poems,* Washington D.C.: Shoemaker & Hoard,

2005. "*(Sunday, July 4)*" from *Sabbaths: Poems,* San Francisco: North Point, 1987. Used by permission of the author.

Budbill, David. "Always in These Ancient Chinese Paintings," "Such Self-Indulgence and Sloth!" "What Issa Heard," and "Quoting T'ao Ch'ien" from *Moment to Moment: Poems of a Mountain Recluse,* Port Townsend, Wash.: Copper Canyon. Copyright © by David Budbill. Reprinted with the permission of Copper Canyon Press, www.copper canyonpress.org.

Cardiff, Gladys. "Where Fire Burns" from *That's What She Said: Contemporary Poetry and Fiction by Native American Women,* edited by Rayna Green. Bloomington and Indianapolis: Indiana University Press, 1984. Reprinted by permission of the author.

Carruth, Hayden. "Particularity" and "The Brook" from *Scrambled Eggs and Whiskey: Poems, 1991–1995,* Port Townsend, Wash.: Copper Canyon. Copyright © 1996 by Hayden Carruth. Reprinted with the permission of Copper Canyon Press, www.coppercanyonpress .org. "The Ravine," "The Poet," and "Of Distress Being Humiliated by the Classical Chinese Poets" from *Toward the Distant Islands: New and Selected Poems,* Port Townsend, Wash.: Copper Canyon. Copyright © 2006 by Hayden Carruth. Reprinted with the permission of Copper Canyon Press, www.coppercanyonpress.org.

Hall, James Baker. "Welcoming the Season's First Insects" and "Kneeling at Easter to the Season's First Bloodroot" from *Stopping on the Edge to Wave,* Middletown, Conn.: Wesleyan University Press, 1988. "The Buffalo" from *The Mother on the Other Side of the World: Poems,* Louisville, Ky.: Sarabande Books, 1999. All poems reprinted by permission of the author.

Han Shan (Cold Mountain). "I delight in the everyday Way, myself," "I've lived out tens of thousands of years," and "The cloud road's choked with deep mist," translated by David Hinton, from *Mountain Home: The Wilderness Poetry of Ancient China,* New York: New Directions. Copyright © 2002, 2005 by David Hinton. Reprinted by permission of New Directions Publishing Corp.

Frost, Robert. "The Oven Bird" originally appeared in *Mountain Interval.* New York: Henry Holt, 1921.

Kenyon, Jane. "February: Thinking of Flowers" and "With the Dog at Sunrise" from *Collected Poems,* Saint Paul, Minn.: Graywolf. Copyright 2005 by the Estate of Jane Kenyon. Reprinted with the permission of Graywolf Press.

Lane, John. "The Homecoming of Osceola" and "The River Falling" from *As the World Around Us Sleeps,* Charlotte, N.C.: Briarpatch Press, 1991. Reprinted by permission of the author.

Levertov, Denise. "Tragic Error" from *Evening Train,* New York: New Directions. Copyright © 1992 by Denise Levertov. Reprinted by permission of New Directions Publishing Corp. "The Life of Others" from *Poems 1972–1982,* New York: New Directions. Copyright © 1978 by Denise Levertov. Reprinted by permission of New Directions Publishing Corp. "The Coming Fall" from *Poems 1960–1967,* New York: New Directions. Copyright © 1964 by Denise Levertov. Reprinted by permission of New Directions Publishing Corp.

Li Po. "Listening to Lu Tzu-Hsün Play the *Ch'in* on a Moonlit Night," "Gazing at the Thatch-Hut Mountain Waterfall," and "Listening to a Monk's *Ch'in* Depths," translated by David Hinton, from *The Selected*

Poems of Li Po, New York: New Directions. Copyright © 1996 by David Hinton. Reprinted by permission of New Directions Publishing Corp.

McCombs, Davis. "Ponds," "Flowstone," and "The River and Under the River" from *Ultima Thule,* New Haven: Yale University Press, 2000. Reprinted by permission of the author.

Miller, Jim Wayne. "Going to Sleep by a Troutstream," "Shapes," and "Winter Days" from *The Brier Poems* by Jim Wayne Miller, Frankfort, Ky.: Gnomon Press. Reprinted by permission of Gnomon Press.

Moeckel, Thorpe. "Bartram's Trail," "Fern," "Bolin Creek," and "On Being Eaten" from *Odd Botany* by Thorpe Moeckel, Eugene, Ore.: Silverfish Review Press. © 2002 by Silverfish Review Press. Reprinted by permission of Silverfish Review Press.

Niedecker, Lorine. "Black Hawk held: In reason," "July, waxwings," "The death of my poor father," and "He lived—childhood summers" from *Lorine Niedecker: Collected Works,* Berkeley, Calif.: University of California Press. © 2002 by the University of California Press.

Oliver, Mary. "The Summer Day" from *New and Selected Poems,* Boston: Beacon Press, 1992. "Sleeping in the Forest" from *Twelve Moons,* Boston: Little Brown and Co., 1979. "The Old Poets of China" from *Why I Wake Early,* Boston: Beacon Press, 2004.

Still, James. "When the Dulcimers Are Gone," "Wilderness," "Heritage," "I Was Born Humble," "Hill-Lonely," "Epitaph for Uncle Ira Combs, Mountain Preacher," and "River of Earth" from *From the*

Mountain, From the Valley, Lexington, Ky.: University Press of Kentucky, 2005.

Taylor, Richard. "Dreaming the Buffalo Back" and "Inventorying Wildflowers along Grindstone Creek on Derby Day" from *Stone Eye,* Monterey, Ky.: Larkspur Press, 2001. "Premises" from *Earth Bones,* Frankfort, Ky.: Gnomon Press, 1979. All poems reprinted by permission of the author.

Tu Fu. "Written on the Wall at Chang's Hermitage," translated by Kenneth Rexroth, from *One Hundred Poems from the Chinese,* New York: New Directions. Copyright © 1971 by Kenneth Rexroth. Reprinted by permission of New Directions Publishing Corp. "Reflections in Autumn," translated by David Hinton, from *The Selected Poems of Tu Fu,* New York: New Directions. Copyright © 1988, 1989 by David Hinton. Reprinted by permission of New Directions Publishing Corp. "Dawn Landscape," translated by David Hinton, from *Mountain Home: The Wilderness Poetry of Ancient China,* New York: New Directions. Copyright © 2002, 2005 by David Hinton. Reprinted by permission of New Directions Publishing Corp.

Wang Wei. "In Reply to Vice-Magistrate Chang," translated by David Hinton, from *Mountain Home: The Wilderness Poetry of Ancient China*, New York: New Directions. Copyright © 2002, 2005 by David Hinton. Reprinted by permission of New Directions Publishing Corp. "Bird and Waterfall Music," translated by Kenneth Rexroth, from *One Hundred More Poems from the Chinese,* New York: New Directions. Copyright © 1970 by Kenneth Rexroth. Reprinted by permission of New Directions Publishing Corp. "With Friends on Shen's Sutra-Study Terrace, New Bamboo Sprouting," translated by David Hinton,